Memories of the Prairie and other Stories

A McLEOD FAMILY MEMOIR

Memories of the Prairie and other Stories

JANET McLEOD

MORTAL
INK PRESS
HERITAGE

MEMORIES OF THE PRAIRIE AND OTHER STORIES
Copyright © 2020 by Elaine McLeod Blake, Margaret McLeod Ebert
and Karen McLeod Cox.

All rights reserved. No part of this book may be used or reproduced
in any manner whatsoever without written permission from the
publisher, except as permitted by U.S. copyright law.
For information, please contact Mortal Ink Press LLC,
PO Box 30811, Raleigh, NC 27622-0811, USA.
www.mortalinkpress.com

Cover design by Sandra L. Vasher / Mortal Ink Press Heritage.

ISBN: 978-1-950989-21-8

DEDICATION

This collection of writings has been compiled by The McLeod Aunts for the benefit of the descendants of Janet and Malcolm McLeod. It is dedicated to the happy times in the Big House on Common Road, where the corn grew tall, maple and apple trees flourished, flowers tossed in the breeze and the elderberry bush by the kitchen window lives on in memory.

March 2020

Janet Ross, High School Graduation Picture.

*The artwork featured on the cover was painted
by Janet herself, a true creative spirit.*

INTRODUCTION

These are the writings of our mother, Janet McLeod. They are the renderings of a happy childhood, during a special time and place in history. Mother was in her late seventies when she recorded these remembrances. That little golden-haired girl about whom she wrote grew up to become a woman who lived a life filled with happiness, but who also experienced times of deep grief. She was grounded in faith. She never lost her love of nature and music or her respect for education and hard work. She carried a profound belief in the good of all humankind. The lessons she learned on the prairie sustained her throughout her life.

Elaine McLeod Blake
Margaret McLeod Ebert
Karen McLeod Cox
November 2019

CONTENTS

MEMORIES OF THE PRAIRIE
1

POETRY
62

STORIES ABOUT MY FATHER
73

THE McLEOD HERITAGE
84

THE STORY OF MY LIFE
97

BIOGRAPHY OF JANET McLEOD
103

CHILDREN OF JANET AND MALCOLM McLEOD
106

ACKNOWLEDGEMENTS
109

MEMORIES OF THE PRAIRIE

MEMORIES OF THE PRAIRIE

I am the child of pioneers. I was born in what was then the British Northwest Territories, before part of that area became the Province of Saskatchewan in the Dominion of Canada.

The North American Prairie is familiar in songs and stories of settlers heading west to find new homes in that great expanse of land populated by native people-Indians they were called-and buffalo, black bear, beaver, wolves and all other wildlife it sustained.

I write about my own unique prairie. It was farther north, colder in winter, spring came later and the grasses were not so tall as in more southern climates.

The horizon came down to meet the earth. The sun rose flat-faced out of the ground in a crimson glare and all the eastern sky was brilliant in its glow. As far as the eye could see there was this vast expanse of unbroken plain, greening under the melting snow. The pale purplish-blue anemones added their humble beauty. Oh, how lovely for a little child to gather! Many I picked for my mother.

We were not bereft of trees. The white poplar grew in bluffs where ever there were low spots where rain could gather.

We children had fantasies of buffalo scratching their backs on the lower branches, or their sides on the trunks. There was little concrete evidence that buffalo had existed, except what was left of their wallows.

Our buffalo wallow was an indentation in the ground about fifteen to twenty feet long and about twelve feet wide. The grass had grown over its basin shape and none of the mud was left in which they rolled to cleanse their hides. The buffalo were gone.

The little gophers whistled and played about their holes; pitiful contrast to what had been.

Then, of course, there was the Texas Sage, we called it wolf willow, in which we thought the wolves hid. This shrub grew sporadically all over, its silver foliage offering a welcome change to the landscape.

It would seem reasonable to believe that the coyotes did make use of all available hiding places as their coats were shades of gray similar to the sage brush. On a clear night when the sun had set and the owls had ceased their hooting, the pervasive silence might be suddenly broken by a few loud yelps, then more answering howls till the whole pack joined in a cacophony of howling, yelping, piercing, pleading, sharp derisive sounds. It was not melodious. We shivered in our beds.

The yard dogs, not to be outdone, set up a barking and howling response, but they stayed quite close to the buildings and although many times the wild beasts seemed to be quite close, there were never any encounters.

Barnyard fowl was often missing but that was one of the trials of homesteading.

The prairie boasts extremities of weather, but the winters are renowned for depths of snow and the short days.

Cold dominates all else. The bright sunshine makes no impression on the freezing temperature. One of nature's ironies is the sight of breath freezing as it leaves the nostrils of all living creatures.

Snow comes early, most always in October and remains till May. Before the slow melting begins in late February or early March, the ground is covered by up to five feet or more in many areas, with great banks of it against the brush. The winds take care of that.

There is nothing more breathtaking than the great expanse of shining whiteness broken only by gray shadows of the drifts and darker shadows of the bushes and the always moving shadows of the eternally drifting clouds.

The feathery white clouds against the clear blue sky is a phenomenon of the Western plains from Oklahoma to the far North.

I have experienced "The winds come howling down the plain", as the song says, but in the wintertime, they were painful to endure. The pioneers survived and built two nations.

EARLIEST MEMORIES

1904-1905

The most long-ago incident I recall is sitting in a highchair outside, loving the sunshine. I was singing so my father said. In those days, I sang a lot, especially in the sunshine. Sunshine was so comforting it warmed me, and made me happy; it still does. My father patted my head, "Are you my baby Edith with the golden hair?" I cannot remember answering. I don't think I could talk.

When I began to get cold or hungry, my mother must have taken me in.

It was dark inside. The one window to the south let in all the light we had. There was an old black cook stove, a table and a bench which was our furniture except for two beds behind a long curtain stretched between two walls to make a bedroom. Of course, there had to be an oil lamp especially for winter. Winter nights were long, very long.

At age three, I was allowed to go out on my own. The poplar bushes around were sparse; no place to get lost. The wide clearing to the South beckoned me. There, the sunshine seemed brighter. The pale blue croci spread in patches among the long green grass no taller than a shag carpet. So, I wandered, conscious of my golden hair blowing around my face and the wonderful warm sunshine.

My favorite resting place was a flat stone, slightly hollowed and very smooth. There I sat and sang. At other times my rag doll came, carried mostly by one stubby arm, grasped in my left hand and dragged along. She was not too important to me because even at that young age, I knew she was not pretty. Unconsciously, I yearned for beauty.

My brother had the iron replica of a locomotive: tall smoke stack, axle, wheels, et al. Mother tied a string on the cow catcher and oh, the power my little being achieved, dragging those wheels behind me. Walking, not looking back, it seemed important that the thing was mostly on its side. Being iron, it did get heavy.

Memory on that day of my brothers, Colin, three years older and Alex, aged eight, are scarce, except for Alex's distress and complaints that, "the baby is ruining my engine". I felt a little badly, too, that the finish became a bit less shiny. It was certainly not ruined. Iron was too tough and that toy was around for years.

ANOTHER EARLY MEMORY

Another early memory takes place in winter. About time for the spring break up [the ice and snow melt], my parents went on a short trip, something to do about a team of horses. After that there was a matched pair of grays called Jack and Jean in the barn.

This must have occurred after my sister Phemie was born, and they must have taken her with them, as I was left at home with the boys, my first experience being separated from my mother for any length of time. My brothers must have been having great times in the barn. Once in a while, Colin burst into the house with an arm load of wood and stoked the stove. I was never cold; if hungry, I forget.

The second afternoon dragged on. I thought about the cans and bottles on a high shelf. Dragging a chair close I climbed and reached a can, also a bottle of brown liquid. With a little banging the lid of the can came off. The candied half orange skins with the hard sugar inside were there for the taking. I ate that lovely sugar and much of the orange peel. To this day, I will say, if offered, "No, not if it contains orange peel, thank you". The bottle enticed me. The lid came off with the first turn. Putting it to my lips, I drank it.

There is no recollection of feeling sick. I took an egg cup and a large cork from the table, filled the egg cup from the water pail and, reaching down a dish towel, inserted some cloth into the egg cup. Then, putting the cork in the water, and putting forefinger and thumb around the cloth draped around the cup, pulled it taut. The cork gradually rose with the towel and fell sidewise. All I wanted was that cork to sit firmly on that cloth. Trying and trying and becoming more frustrated every time, I was near to tears, when, finally, the cork was straight in the water and I began to exult. Crash, a hand came down on the cork, water splashed, disaster! Colin had come in with his occasional arm load of wood, and done the dastardly trick. After that I remember lying on the board floor screaming and kicking till I was exhausted. When our mum got home, Colin told her I drank all the vanilla and got drunk. No one has accused me of anything similar since.

It was a good thing mother and dad took the trip to purchase them, because Jack and Jean were around for a long time. They took us on all the winter outings, and pulled the plow, harrow and reaper in summer. And I survived my brothers' baby sitting with no lasting harm!

THE PAISLEY SHAWL

1904

My mother's shawl was a large square of very fine beige wool with a brown paisley pattern all over and a long soft brown fringe. This lovely material, hand woven in India, was used as a scarf on my mother's grand piano back in Scotland.

I remember one late evening being taken from my parents' bed and waking just as I was being tucked snuggly among pillows and blankets on top of a large box, the kind used to ship house hold goods across the ocean and, subsequently, for storage.

In the dim light of the coal oil lamp, it seemed to my three-year-old sight a long way to the floor. I was lonely. The first emotion I remember feeling was that I had a dire fear of falling to the boarded floor. I do not remember crying. The neighbor who was caring for me was kind and I was warm. There was activity on the other side of the blanket hung across the opening into where my parents slept. The neighbor, Mrs. Baugh, passed back and forth to the kitchen stove on some unknown errand. Of the mysterious activities, I had no comprehension. Next in memory is the bright morning sun lighting up our window. I was sitting by the stove alone. The woman had gone.

My father appeared from outside, letting in a wintry blast. He carried what appeared to be my rag doll wrapped in Mum's paisley shawl and with a sheepish grin went into where she was. They called me to see my new baby sister whom God had left for us. I have no memory of the baby but I do remember wondering why he had my Mum's paisley shawl and why that bundle coming in the door had looked so much like my doll and why the baby who seemed to replace the doll hadn't frozen in the icy snow. It was puzzling.

The other memory of that winter was my mother fussing with food to satisfy the little preemie and keep her alive.

It was a long time before I learned about biological facts, but my little sister Phemie quickly became a loving friend. The paisley shawl that used to cover the baby grand piano in Scotland, found better use on the prairie.

THE BUFFALO WALLOW

The part of the Western plains where I was born did not have the tall grass or deep top soil of which we read in Kansas and farther south. There was enough black loam, however, to produce crops for many years without much thought of replenishing it.

I remember going one cool morning while the dew was still glistening, to pick strawberries. We walked about a half mile in the bright sunshine until we came to a clump of bushes straggling around a clearing where the strawberry patch showed red and white jewels among the green leaves. The strawberries were the sweetest and we had beaten the blackbirds.

I tired of picking and strayed from my mother who was still bending to the ground industriously filling her pail. I was probably four or five. I wandered away and found something wondrous. It was a large hollowed place in the land, just like a giant basin. My mother said it had been a buffalo wallow, but now the grass had grown over it to cover all the signs of those vanishing herds, nothing left but the hollow in the ground. How many herds for how many years had roamed here and scratched their backs and sides on these same scraggly bushes, and wallowed in the coolness of this very earth?

I ran from one edge to the other and played and dreamed. The sun rose high and grew hot and it was time to go. Reluctantly, I took my Mother's hand and we started home. I shall always remember finding the buffalo wallow.

ROBINS

1906

It was a wondrous, beauteous morning. The sun was beginning to climb, providing a full-blown noonday heat. A silent infant breeze cooled my face and ruffled my hair.

I walked along the lane following my father, where his team had traversed much earlier, to begin the spring plowing. He'd been working since dawn.

There was the big, colorless field before me, with two ploughed stretches, yards apart. The team was headed toward me, plowing the right-hand strip.

I waited till they reached the end where my father would edge the plow out of the ground and head his team to the left strip. The plow share dug deep into the earth as the sharp coulter cut into the virgin sod.

The smooth earth was exposed to the sunshine. A comforting, smooth flat furrow, about sixteen inches wide, invited me to follow.

The sun shone on the over turned sod, which was dark brown, smooth and shining. I loved the feel of the earth on my bare feet. I followed my father's back as he steered the team, producing a straight, long stretch of ground falling exactly on the edge of the turned-up sod beside it.

I was not alone following the ploughing. The robins were all around, probably grateful for the worms the plow share uncovered. I watched them as they alighted, swiftly cocked their heads and struck with their bills at the delightful smorgasbord so easily available. There were other birds, but none so bold as the robins.

Sometime in August, the wheat was ripened. I again followed my father to the field to watch him begin the harvest. The first procedure was to activate the binder; this horse drawn machine had been a godsend to the farmers. As the horses drew it along, a sharp blade carried great swatches of grain. A canvas conveyer carried it up and into the machine where by some ingenious method it was bundled, batch after batch, into sheaves and tossed on the stubby ground.

But back to the robins. As my father lifted the binder twine lid to install the spool of twine, a very frightened and angry robin flew out. There was her nest! The young ones, partially feathered, stretched their necks with wide open mouths. Poor little things! My father was as disconsolate as I. What to do? The harvest had to begin.

We gently gathered the nest, together with all the babies in it, and placed it on the ground under the nearest bush. We thought the mother would surely find them.

I worried about those robins and how they would survive. As of now, I know more about robins, and am certain they did.

SCHOOL DAYS

CLUMBER SCHOOL

1908

The area of the British Northwest Territories where we lived had been surveyed and plotted into six mile by six-mile districts. This meant each one contained thirty-six, one square mile sections. Each divided into four produced a homestead site a quarter mile square.

Not until enough settlers took up land claiming their allotted quarter section would the districts be named. In 1908, when my school life began, the district was called Clumber after an area in Northumberland from which the Bird family on the adjoining quarter had come. I have no data to corroborate this except my memory, and I knew Mr. and Mrs. Bird well. Their accent spoke heavily of the north of England. My family, the Rosses, had homesteaded on the Southwest Quarter, Section Two, Range One, West of Second Meridian. Sensibly enough, the school building had been placed close to the center of the District. This meant that to get to school we would walk over three miles each way.

Starting out each morning with my two brothers was a pleasant experience. The bushes between the house and the valley bank were alive with blackbirds, thousands of them, we thought. How they sang! I shall never forget that music so sweet on the fresh morning air.

We pretended the valley bank gave us a head start as we ran down its steep slope, my brothers Alex, Colin and I. The other side was a gentle swell to level ground where we walked kitty-corner across the section toward the creek bank. This ground was not yet cultivated because it was very stony.

In spring and late summer there was, to our right, "The Big Slough". Surrounded by reeds and grasses, it was the home of frogs, toads and myriad crawling creatures, mud hens, and ducks. We knew the mallard, teal, bittern, canvasback and pintail well. The slough was really a very large pond and a wonderful breeding ground for water-fowl.

But back to getting to school. We did not dawdle as we played a game we called catch up. One would race ahead of the others who then vied to be first to reach the one ahead. Growing tired of that, we jumped from stone to stone trying not to step on the ground, but of course that was an impossibility.

This area was not ploughed until modern farming equipment came into use. When I visited many years later, one enormous wheat field met my view. Gone were the stones, wolf willow, golden lady slippers and even the big slough. It had never recovered from the drought years of the thirties. I feel a twinge of sadness as I write.

But on to school. Down the banks of Cut Arm Creek, across the meadow onto the narrow, Macadamized road we went, and crossed the wooden bridge over that clear, lovely creek. A long walk on the other side, up the steep bank, and we were at Clumber School.

Outside, the building was like all the others we sometimes see today, preserved but empty, along the highways as we travel. Ours faced North with an attached coat and mud room entrance. Inside, the double desks placed in rows on each side of the room were fastened firmly to the floor without regard for comfort. On the East wall hung a map of Canada, covering a great space, beside a picture of the then reigning monarch and his queen. At that time, it must have been Edward and Alexandra. I am not sure, but I still see that map of Canada in my mind's eye. I could draw it today. North, South, East and West were embedded in my memory.

On the opposite wall, four large windows looked out across the pasture to a large gully running down to the creek, which had woods beyond. Cattle grazed and turkeys, escaped from some barnyard, frequently ran about. Watching them was a welcome relief from the often boredom of the classroom.

A raised platform across the entire front accommodated the teacher's desk and chair, which sat in the center. The same familiar blackboard with which we are today familiar adorned the back wall, only ours was made of slate. How easily the chalk slipped across it! At one end there were bookshelves containing our small lending library. How fortunate for us that someone had thought of the necessity of books other than textbooks. "The Tale of Bunny Cottontail" was the first one I read.

I must not forget to mention our heating facility. It was a large box stove made of iron and sat in the middle of the room. It had an ordinary stovepipe going up through the roof. The teacher kept it stoked with proper lengths of wood provided by the trustees. In later years, a more modern heater, with a circular enclosure of shiny metal was installed. It was much safer and somewhat more attractive and the heat was distributed more evenly so the closest to it were not scorching while the farthest away were chilled.

Our sanitary facilities were, of course, two neat little houses, one on the right side far corner of the fenced yard for the boys, and one on the left corner for the girls. There I had my first sight of graffiti scrawled by one of the older girls. To my innocent mind it was vulgar and shocking and I would never repeat it. But it did rhyme and I still remember that jingle.

In the cloakroom sat a bench on which was a large granite pail with a dipper to match, for our drinking water. There must have been a basin for handwashing but I don't recall one. No one brought their own cup; everyone used the dipper. The water came from the well that was at the bottom of the hill, beside the road. Each day, two of the largest boys took turns carrying the full pail up the hill. A hard job, but I used to envy them the fun of running down the hill during school hours to fill it. I always loved running down hills.

Our teachers were a conglomeration, a different one every season. The first years they were all males; young men from the universities earning their way during the summer break. I still see the blackboard, one term, on which was drawn the diagram, in large scale, of a red heart, with aorta, arteries, and veins. They were all colored and named and the medical student teacher was using it to lecture the three or four older pupils. It happened on the day the school inspector came, and I heard him ask the teacher, "Are some of these going to be doctors"? Then there was Mr. Tripp, the one who loved music. He drew the treble clef on the blackboard and taught us the scale, some little songs and how each note sounded. Music theory. I think that was a first for all of us.

The year my oldest brother was getting ready for eighth grade exams, there must have been English literature requirements. I remember so well the teacher reading Shelly and having the class memorize.

My own work was forgotten as I sat spellbound listening to those lovely poetic words of "To a Skylark".

Hail to thee, blithe spirit
    Bird thou never wert
That from Heaven, or near it,
    Pourest thy full heart
In profuse strains of unpremeditated art……

What thou art we know not;
What is most like thee?……

That was the beginning of my love affair with the English language.

Left to right, Beth, Janet and Phemie Ross, 1909.

AN INTERLUDE

1908-1910

The phrase "the Protestant work ethic" is one that is bandied about loosely and carelessly to stereotype people who believe that work is one of the most essential ingredients in a successful life. In my experience as a child, work was essential to procure even the most rudimentary necessity.

So it was that many children of the first settlers in American and Canadian farm lands were needed at home to help wrest a livelihood from the virgin prairies. Consequently, they received very little schooling.

Attesting to this, in my district, the most seemingly prosperous family had kept their two older daughters at home to work until in their late teens. One summer, surprisingly, they both began to attend school.

Amelia and Clarise Sawyer, called Mimmie and Clary, drove a buggy to school, accompanied by the young bachelor teacher who boarded at their home. Their sister, Olive, was my age and my first school friend. I thought she was the prettiest person in the world and I adored her.

Olive and Amelia shared a desk and Clary and I shared the one behind them. I remember this because Mr. Tripp, our teacher, had very little knowledge of how to teach beginning math, as it is now called. He put long lines of addition problems on the board, and Olive and I were to add them. I always had a wrong answer, even if I finished them. Dear Amelia took pity on us both and quickly gave Olive the answers to both of the problems, and to me she gave one. At least I wasn't completely humiliated.

But that is not the story. It was not long before "little pitcher's with big ears", as I heard remarked, began to hear jokes about a romance between Amelia and Mr. Tripp. There were little innuendoes about why schooling was suddenly so necessary for Amelia. It was the young man teacher that term, a very eligible bachelor, who was boarding with the family.

Time went on for a year or two, and the teacher who boarded at the Sawyer home went back to university. After his departure, the older girls stayed home again to care for their ailing mother and resume their farm labors.

The year Olive and I turned twelve, Mr. Tripp was back teaching for a few months. Now the rumors were rife, surely, he and Mimmie would marry. But they did not.

So, it was all forgotten. Olive and I left school after eighth grade and I went away to high school, while her education was concluded.

A few years later the news broke. Mr. Tripp and Olive were married. Everyone pitied Mimmie but no one knew the whole story.

He became a school inspector and Olive, with her eighth-grade education, became the educator's wife. I had gone to high school and Normal Teacher's Training School, becoming a country school teacher. I married a handsome farmer.

THE BLUE MARE

1910

I remember standing at the inner corner of the lane with my mother when my father appeared leading his new purchase.

She seemed to be of no particular breed but good looking. Not heavy like a work horse nor light like a racer or pony. Her coat was sleek but of a peculiar color, a very light bay with a bluish cast, not anything describable, so my father dubbed her "The Blue Mare".

To my mother's dismay, she seemed to have a limp in her front legs. She exclaimed in astonishment, "That's what he paid two hundred dollars for?"

As they came closer, we saw it was true. The mare had a stiffness in her front quarters. My dad calmly announced, "She's been foundered". What good was a foundered horse?

My father knew and she came through. Throughout the summer the Blue Mare was never harnessed to do any work. She grazed, drank and rested. The limp gradually disappeared. She always received an extra handful of oats from my Dad. Over the winter she was stabled and pampered.

On May fifth, the morning was chilly with a skiff of crunchy snow which had fallen overnight. My father called us to go to the barn. We all crunched out to see what he was so excited about.

There stood the Blue Mare in the straw lined stall

straining her neck to reach with her tongue a lanky, wobbly, long legged foal just barely able to stand on its feet. She licked till her baby was shiny clean.

We were all ecstatic. The newcomer was so pretty. She was definitely a blond bay. Her little tail was curly and bright colored as was the stubby mane.

My father's eyes sparkled with delighted satisfaction. We all cried together, "What shall we name her"? My mother suggested, "Well, it's May and the Hawthorns will be in bloom pretty soon. Why not call her May Blossom?" We all agreed and May Blossom was the beginning of a family of blond bay horses which within three horse generations were pure bred Clydesdales. One matched team took prizes at all the country fairs and my father's Clydesdales, for many years, were known all around the district.

The Blue Mare was vindicated.

BEAVERS

1911

On a sultry Sunday afternoon my sister Phemie and I were restless, fidgety and prone to giggle, upon which our father frowned. Children kept quiet in the house on Sunday. Could a man not read his weekly newspaper in peace?

My mother handed us two clean, half gallon syrup pails and said, "Go find some raspberries for supper".

With swift energy we grasped the pails and set out for the

creek bank. We knew where the usually prolific vines grew. They were part of the tangled undergrowth of a healthy stand of white poplars. It stood on a plateau of the bank leading to the creek.

We ran down the first slope to the edge of the bush. Both stood still in shocked amazement. Something had happened! The raspberry patch was in shambles. Twigs, with leaves intact and fresh cut branches, lay all around. One long, straight poplar, cropped of all branches, lay prone. We noticed the foot-high stump was shaped like a beautifully sharpened lead pencil, smooth and neat. Sharp teeth marks showed evenly. Beavers! What other animal could do such a thing?

This was the material for their dam! A colony was making a new home. The long, large log would have to be rolled to the edge and down the hill, across the meadow to the stream. It would be the support from one edge of the stream to the other. All other branches and twigs would be piled against it. With time, patience and labor, the work would go on. Lesser trees would be cut, dragged, and rolled until the barrier was high and tight. The force of flowing water would help squeeze all compact, until a minimum of flow escaped. The water would grow steadily deeper until the dam was accomplished and a pond in which to build a lodge was formed.

We did not see the beavers. I think they worked early in the morning and late in the evening. I have not lost any of my admiration and respect for those fairly large, brown animals with the beautiful coats.

Phemie and I did find plenty of luscious, bright red berries to take home, but they were not as valuable as the memory of that 'nature scene', and the beauty of that wonderful day.

THE OYSTER SUPPER

1911

It had been a long time since Christmas. The winter was becoming monotonous. The settlers in their far separate homes needed some event to break the constant sameness.

Finally, it came. An Oyster Supper was planned to be held in the school house. There would be food and entertainment, but the main attraction was oyster stew.

My bachelor uncles were part of the committee, so we heard of all that was going on. Excitement! Finally, something different happening! All bundled up, we sat in the sled, Alex, Colin, Phemie and I, along with mother and father. The grey team trotted briskly along the glistening trail across the snow.

In the school house the furnace like stove gave off great comfort. People greeted each other with friendship and laughter. All was pleasant. Supper was announced.

I have no idea where the hot steaming bowls of this famous stew came from; all I remember is my hungry stomach giving a lurch of rejection when a bowl was set before me. A grey looking liquid with a lumpy object floating in the middle and an unfamiliar smell seemed very unappetizing. Adults around me ooh'd and aah'd at the flavor. "Wonderful to have two kegs of frozen oysters all the way from the coast"! Well, good for them. I have never acquired a taste for oysters.

Then came the entertainment. Various people were called upon to contribute what they could. One after another went onto the platform and did recitations, some funny, some sad, told jokes, and sang songs, including one or two of Harry Lauder's most acceptable. Then the chairman called on my mother to close the program by singing.

She stepped onto the platform; a short, slightly rounded lady with great dignity and stage presence. She had been trained as a singer in Scotland.

It must have been near St. Patrick's Day for she sang "The Kerry Dancers", light and lilting. Then "Kathleen Mavourneen", sad and nostalgic. After those, her old Scottish favorites "Ye Banks and Braes o' Bonnie Doon, how can ye bloom so fresh and fair? How can ye chant, ye little bird and I sae weary, full of care?" And then, of course, "Annie Laurie". What Scottish person would not sing "Annie Laurie"?

My mother's voice was renowned in the area, and she was invited to sing at every important gathering in the adjoining districts.

Last summer [1988] members of our family traveled to the small town of Bredenbury, Saskatchewan, where the cousins living there were hosting a family reunion in conjunction with a town birthday celebration.

Margaret, my daughter, having been invited to do so by her cousin, sang at the town church service.

Two or three surviving pioneers were thrilled to hear a voice like the one they remembered from so many years ago. Being told my daughter's singing reminded them of my mother, her grandmother Webster, brought me great joy! But the memory of the oyster stew still makes my stomach blanch.

Editors' Note. At that reunion in Bredenbury, Saskatchewan in 1988, the elderly pioneers who marveled at Margaret's voice, also spoke fondly, if somewhat incredulously, of the Webster family, who came to the prairie from Scotland with musical instruments, silver, china, and a set of Shakespeare. It seemed the unspoken thought was perhaps spades and shovels would have been more appropriate.

BRIDGES

Since we lived east of the Cut Arm Creek and our school was on the top of its west bank, our early school life began by crossing a bridge twice a day. No wonder then that the two bridges of which we had a choice are indelible in my memory.

I want to write about the new one which was built when I was about eight or nine years old. It was called the bridge at "Ross's Crossing", because my aunts were the first white women to ford that stream in 1883.

As we walked home from school, we had an opportunity to stay and watch the contraption called the 'pile driver'. It was a rig secured in the swampy ground somehow and rising thirty or forty feet high. At the top was a strong wheel over which a stronger cable hung. One end of the cable was attached to a solid cylindrical maul. At the other end a team of horses was hitched.

A supply of round timber, probably treated by creosote or some other then known preservative, lay ready to be driven into the ground. After the men had labored to stand a timber upright between the rigging, the team would be driven forward and the maul pulled to the top. Miraculously, some gadget sprung its jaws and the heavy maul sped down to drop with a thud and drive the pile into the ground. This long, tedious process continued until all the piles were in their places.

The next process was to lay the cross beams and floor to the bridge with, to my child's mind, beautiful thick hewn planks.

The day came when the workmen left. As we children came to the beautiful new bridge, how we admired it. We stomped on it to hear the hollow sound it made. Most thrillingly, later, was the tramp of the horses' hooves clanking on the planks and the delightful rattle of the vehicle wheels.

All of the equipment was gone except the pile driver which was on the opposite side of the stream, and a twelve-inch plank that was thrown across the water where the men had crossed back and forth from either side of the stream during construction.

That plank was so tempting. I went down the bank and told my brother I was going to walk across it. He remonstrated, and then walked on leaving me. I stepped gingerly at first then a feeling of elation came over me. I stepped daringly to the middle. The plank was quite bouncy by now. I could see my reflection in the clear, cold water. One more little bounce and my feet hit the bottom of the stream. My pleated, woolen skirt floated up to my armpits and then sank. My bubble had burst! I struggled to the bank and scrambled out; the weight of the soggy material almost too heavy for me. I grasped it piece by piece and tried to wring the water out with little success. So, nothing to do but start walking the two miles home. My shoes were soggy, the skirt heavy and I had to face my mother. At my snail pace the dry breeze and afternoon sunshine lightened my load and when I reached home, I looked almost normal except the beautiful pleats were no longer sharp. In fact, they never were again but, joy of joy, that was my only punishment.

So much for being adventurous. But, that experience did not deter me from another childhood game; climbing the post of a rail fence, gingerly standing on the top rail, tottering with out stretched arms trying to reach the next post. That slender rail rocked down and up at every step. Not often did I triumph. Despite admonishments and skinned knees, I don't remember giving up trying.

NATIVE FRIENDS

A STORY OF TRUST

The Cut Arm Creek was a very wide gorge in the prairie, as geologists would have it, formed by moving ice as the earth began to warm at the end of the Ice Age. Be that as it may, the west end of the section on which we lived was bordered by its steep banks, beautiful meadow and a flowing creek which supported a large colony of beaver and muskrat.

In the autumn, families of Indians traveled along its banks, they pitched their tents, usually in the shelter of a bluff if there was one, and took up residence. If the animals were plentiful, they would soon have their livelihood. They were welcome to them. After they had gone, we children would examine the bare spot their camp left for anything that was there. There was always nothing except the smothered embers where their fires had been.

As new settlers moved in and put up barbed wire fences this custom was abandoned except for a few older Indians.

One couple came so many years in a row that my parents became acquainted with them. They were Mr. and Mrs. Acoose. They were always treated with courtesy. The man would ask my father to buy oats for his pony. He received his bag of oats and no payment was accepted.

When Mrs. Acoose came to the door, my mother asked her in and made her tea and served something to eat. When she left, she would have a home-made loaf, some flour and sugar and maybe some eggs.

I had a little "come late" brother who refused to wear shoes except in winter. When he was two or three, he liked to go into the bush, disrobe and come out bare, much to the consternation of anyone present! Mrs. Acoose returned after seeing one of these exhibitions with a beautifully beaded pair of buckskin moccasins. She handed them to my mother, shaking her head disapprovingly and protesting, "Papoose! No good bare feet!". My mother accepted them with thanks. When my father came in, he took the moccasins and hung them on the wall saying they were too pretty to wear and get dirty. They were still hanging up when I went away to school two years later. One time she brought beautifully tanned black calfskin also for the papoose.

The last time I saw them was at a Sunday dinner. Mrs. Acoose had accepted the invitation to eat with us as she had come, I am sure inadvertently, at dinner time. Probably she thought it would be rude to refuse. She was bashful and uncomfortable with so many present. The white tablecloth and silver may have been a culture shock. There was no conversation as she had still very few English words. After that day, Mr. and Mrs. Acoose never came back. Probably they were too old to hunt and dig for root anymore.

The memorable thing is, our parents taught us a vivid lesson in tolerance, acceptance of people who were different, and above all, forgiveness. It had been only twenty years since my father had joined the Army of "Red Coats" to quell an Indian uprising known as the Riel Rebellion, named for Louis Riel, the Indian who led it.

THE CORSET

My mother had a sister, Aunt Euphemia, who married an established farmer near Winnipeg. Winnipeg had been settled quite a few years before my father's homestead. That explains their seeming prosperity.

It was Aunt Euphemia's custom to send packages of clothing to us and, if there was anything suitable, we probably used it. None of it was anything memorable except for one thing. That was a corset! The contraption had an hourglass shape and plenty of boning. I immediately recognized it as the thing that made all those shapely models in the catalogs look the way they looked. How I admired them. I asked mum if I could wear the corset to the upcoming picnic.

Well, I wore it. It pinched my waist and was a little loose on my preadolescent hips. With my leg-horn hat adorned with some ribbons and my white dotted-swiss dress, I looked like—anyway a little like—the ladies in the catalog. I thought I looked glamorous as I sauntered around the picnic grounds. I had not yet sat down!

The picnic games began. At the age of twelve and a half, I thought it would be beneath my dignity to run races carrying eggs on a teaspoon or join a sack race. Finally, the potato race came along. I was being persuaded, pushed, even bullied into joining some game, so at the potato race I gave in.

My partner was Ned, a gangling youth about fifteen and known for his slow learning ability. That was a handicap to begin with. The potatoes were arranged in lines about five or six feet apart and the contestants had to pick one up, run to the next and so on. I forget how it really went. What I do remember is bending down. I couldn't! The steel in the front of the contraption I was wearing stuck in my pelvic bone at the bottom, and in my rib cage at the top. I was in a strait jacket. I kept on trying. Every potato reached was agony. Everyone watching wondered why a slender girl would be so slow. Ted and I finished last!

In every other way it was a pleasant picnic. There were more games in which I did not participate. There was plenty of wonderful food and at the end, ice cream, wonder of wonders. Back home, the corset was consigned to oblivion. As far as I was concerned, I would wait and let my body take its own shape.

SCHOOL DAYS

CHURCHBRIDGE

1916-1917

The school year after eighth grade my brother Colin and I drove a team and sled to the new school in Bredenbury, Saskatchewan which boasted two levels, with four classrooms on each. The lower floor housed two teachers and all of the students in the elementary grades one through eight. One upper classroom took care of the ninth graders. The fourth would continue empty until the next year when, it was hoped, there would be enough pupils to fill the space.

This was an unrealistic projection, especially in war time. Until that was over, few farmers could afford to spare any child from the myriad chores necessary to the production of extra crops.

The town of Churchbridge had also built a similar school building, and it was decided arrangements would be made for me to be sent there the next year. So it was, at age fourteen, entering ninth grade, my home was with a Danish lady. I say lady advisedly. No other word in my vocabulary can more aptly describe her poise, gentleness and restraint in her sometimes-trying position as the wife of an Icelandic prairie businessman. That the Danes were far superior to peoples of the other Nordic cultures, she never forgot.

At no time did she enter the general store where Barney Westman, her husband, spent most of his working hours. He must have made a satisfactory living, as there were only two stores in town or for many miles around. His was a truly country store. Dark, dusty, wide board flooring, and shelves, counters, and open barrels crammed with every kind of merchandise from needles to bolts of material to food.

My interest lay in the barrels, at times filled, and at other times nearly empty, with among other items, bread, rolls, hardtack, dried apples, figs, raisins, and smoked, dried herring. All looked delicious, except for the herring. Oh, those fish! That smell! Was it pungent or malodorous? Maybe a little of both.

After being close to them, I hurriedly bought my patty of solidified maple sugar, went back to my room and enjoyed it, not mindful if I had picked up the odor on my clothing or whether that crunchy sweetness was clean.

The neat little town of Churchbridge clung to the Canadian Pacific Railway, it seemed, by its tiny red station house. I remember it as being plain and lonesome all during the week, truly a farmer's town. Saturday it came alive. The livery stable was full. All sorts of vehicles came and went. The Post Office and stores were busy. People stood in groups and talked. Sundays were also different and therein lies my tale, but back to the Westmans and my schooling.

The large, sparsely furnished room behind the store served as a dining and sitting room. There I did my homework. My bedroom upstairs was too lonely.

My struggle to get through "Ivanhoe" turned me from Sir Walter Scott forever, except for "The Lady of the Lake" and the other of his poetry. There was plenty of required reading to keep me occupied, as well as mathematics, grammar, lots of grammar, and poetry memorization. And of course, I can't leave out my study of good old British history.

Mrs. Westman, as soon as possible after every meal, returned to her beautifully furnished sitting room above the store.

Sundays were different. That bare room served as a reception hall for every farmer from the Iceland Colony north of town. They came prepared to spend the day at Westman's store or in his home. Around twelve noon the big cups, rolls and lumps of sugar appeared. Mrs. Westman poured large pots of coffee. The men straggled in from the cold and sat around the table talking constantly in Icelandic. Mr. Barney Westman ceremoniously joined them, placing two large bottles of whiskey firmly on each end of the table. Strong, hot coffee laced with liquor accompanied with lumps of sugar warmed their spirts as well as their bodies. Probably the only break in their dreary lives.

Mrs. Westman spoke to no one. She served them seemingly with repressed disdain and appeared pleased when the last one left.

Once or twice a month in the fall, my father came to take me home for the week end and to pay my board and room. Those were happy times for me when I was able to go home, because I missed my family and being shy and a stranger in town, found it hard to make new friends.

One friend I did make, however, was Margaret Hall. She lived on a farm, a half mile from the school house and we became close. Later her younger brother, Harold, and my sister Beth married. I saw her two years ago. She too had been a country school teacher. We had a great reunion.

Nineteen fifteen's winter was bitter cold. My trips home were not frequent which enabled me to be a part of a memorable activity in the community.

The Churchbridge community was indeed a melting pot. On the North were the Icelanders. South and East, a German colony and scattered families of Norwegians, Swedes, and second-generation Americans from the Dakotas, Minnesota and Michigan.

Some dedicated people decided that since there was no church in town, something on a religious order should be organized. So, it was every Sunday morning a Sunday School class would convene in the town hall. This was a large frame edifice warmed by a stove and furnished with chairs and a table or two.

At Mrs. Westman's suggestion I attended the opening. After that, every Sunday saw me there until springtime. It was not school; there were no classes. It was not church; there was no preacher or preaching that remains in my memory. There were songbooks, a piano and singing. Whether it was tuneful, I do not know. To the fact that it was loud and enthusiastic, I can still attest because sides were chosen for hymn singing. The Reds and Blues contested which would bring the most participants. The place soon bulged. No matter they had to arise in the darkness to breakfast, care for their stock, and ready themselves and their children for mostly long cold drives, they came.

The cold hall soon warmed. The odor of snow melting on heavy boots and damp woolen clothing permeated the air. A muted carnival spirit seemed to exist. Fathers, mothers and children sat in rows, the Reds and Blues on opposite sides of the aisle. The leader read from Scriptures and there was some discussion I do not remember. The singing began. Hymn after hymn was chosen and sung with gusto. The meeting must have closed with prayer. The people dispersed to their homes after the women had visited. The men hitched the teams and brought the sleighs to the door. Then it was home to their lonely farms.

Why had they come? Why spend so much effort for one brief span of human companionship? Perhaps for the adults it was a nostalgic trip back to their childhoods of comfortable homes where religion was taught and there were churches to attend in a climate not so harsh. Or could it be that the hymn singing was a catharsis for their disappointments, frustrations, and tensions in their struggle to conquer a new land? Probably they could not have told.

It must be assumed, however, because of the gathering, that their homes would be more loving and harmonious. The trips to "Sunday School" provided enough joy to outweigh the trouble it took to get there, or they would not have continued their faithful attendance.

MY PONY

1913

When I see stories in the newspapers of unrest and violence still plaguing Ireland, I am reminded of an Irishman who frequently visited my home.

He was a welcome guest because he was well read and seemed to be informed of the current events in the world at

Janet and her younger sister, Beth, 1913.

that time. He liked children and brought me books to read. Some of them I really did not like. They were moralist and Pollyanna-ish. The girl heroines did a lot of crying and being sorry for their minor infractions. My first experience with chauvinism.

Mr. Hartford talked a lot about his homeland; one would wonder why he had left! Maybe some type of political trouble. He mentioned the "Sinn Feiners" often. They were the organization of revolutionary Roman Catholics who are probably the IRA of today. He spoke of boys and men carrying shillelaghs: oaken sapling rods, or stones in a stocking, lacking the oak, which was meant to protect themselves or to attack others. Much less deadly than the guns of today but quite as brutal.

I don't remember just quite how old I was when he brought a pony for us to keep. This was supposed to be a loan so I could have a horse of my own. I was no horse lover and it was the first inkling I had that I was supposed to learn to ride.

The pony was white with an oversized head and certainly slightly homely. I'm sure he was old and I know he had a hard mouth, as he was slow to respond to the tug of an ordinary bit. And he was ornery. His name was Larry Doolan.

The beast was bridled and saddled. I bravely climbed onto his back and persuaded him to go. He went at his own gait and where he wished, mostly. Once when I was going for the cows, we had occasion to get them out of the bush. What an opportunity for Larry Doolan to rid himself of the nuisance on his back. He went straight for the lowest tree with a low hanging branch. I yanked on the reigns, but he would not stop. The branch just came level with my chin but was very supple and bent far back. I stayed mounted with only an abrasion!

Winter came and it became too cold for me to ride. I never did become compatible with Larry Doolan. My sister, Phemie, who liked to ride, took over his care.

Larry Doolan and Mr. Hartford.

THE VALLEY

"I chatter, chatter as I flow
To join the brimming river
For men may come and men may go,
But I go on forever".

So said Tennyson in his poem "The Brook"

The brook of my memory did not go on forever. It flowed and chattered only while the snow on its banks melted to water, racing through its narrow bed. It seemed that a giant flour scoop has taken a gouge out of the flat prairie and left a stretch of fairly steep bank on the east and a gentle sloping one on the west. "The Valley" was our family's name for this pleasant area.

Waking early, hearing the sound of rushing water was a feeling akin to Christmas. "The Valley is running! The Valley is running!" were shouts of joy. The winter at last was over.

If the snow had been deep, and drifted into banks, the water gurgled and roared struggling down to find its level and join the Cut Arm Creek.

Where it went, we did not care. We loved to play around that stream. Boat racing was very popular. Smooth dried sticks were our boats. They were light and traveled fast on the water as we ran along beside trying to keep our shoes dry; hopeless task.

As weather warmed the stream narrowed. Now it was time to doff our shoes and stockings and attempt our yearly dam building. What a chore! If our parents had asked us to work so hard, we would have been very unwilling.

Ah, but Phemie and I would have liked to keep that stream which had started to become narrower and less deep. We gathered stones small and large as we could carry, dropped them side by side across the, by now, gently flowing water bed. It took so many stones! They became heavier as we worked. The task started to appear hopeless. The water still got through. Anyway, it had been fun, and there was always tomorrow.

Tomorrow and the stream was barely dampening the stone's tops. A few small ones and some sticks began to hold some of the water making a little basin. We had succeeded at least partially and I have no recollection of anything but happy feelings about it.

In a few days the stream was a trickle. The snow had melted and there were summer adventures to plan.

Editors' Note. Janet loved poetry. Alfred Lord Tennyson was among her favorite poets. She memorized "The Brook" at an early age, and recited it often all of her life.

CHRISTMAS ON THE PRAIRIE

The pattern of Christmas repeated for years while I was very young.

For days in December before the longed-for day arrived there was cleaning and polishing every little piece of household ornament brought lovingly from the "Old Country". [Scotland] Those little touches of beauty brought gladness to my heart. I can't ever forget the curtains, lovely, lacy patterns stretched, stiffly starched, hanging in front of the ice-covered window pane, and without, the sun glinting on the mounds of pure white snow.

Preparing the Christmas pudding was truly a work of art. All those luscious fruits and candied peel, suet and eggs, mixed to just the right consistency to be formed into a large ball, and piled into a well washed empty sugar sack. Then, "plop" into the enormous kettle to boil and bubble as long as Dad kept the fire stoked.

Then, after days of making the shortbread, the fruit cakes, the mince pies, preparing the fowl and all that went with it, it was finally time for fun.

Our bachelor uncles were our most looked for guests. They got the Glasgow papers, and all the news from "home" was discussed; especially about the football [soccer] teams, the game scores, etc.

Then the feast! How we ate. No one said "Grace". We all stood and sang the Doxology, "Praise God from Whom all Blessings Flow". My mother's sweet clear soprano seemed to envelope us all and I think in our hearts we all praised Him.

It was not long till we children wanted our best treats. Someone would say "Uncle Henry, play the flute", which he gladly did. Then "Uncle Colin, play the whistle". He played simple ditties which all sang. Uncle Andrew played the mouth organ and wonder of wonders, Uncle Andrew danced the sword dance, the Highland Fling and parts of reels; things he had learned in dancing school. [In Scotland.] Then, oh joy, my mother sang. "Ye Banks and Braes o'Bonnie Doone", "Bonnie Charles No Awa", "The Bonnie, Banks O'Loch Lomond", "There were Ninety and Nine", "Kilarney", and some old Scottish Psalms. No one noticed the time and we were not sent to bed until we could no longer sit up. It was warm and quiet in our upstairs and the pleasant sound of adults talking soon lulled us to sleep.

In later years, Uncle Colin learned to play the violin and Mother sang with him.

ONE SPECIAL CHRISTMAS

1910

One special Christmas gathering in my home, which stands out among them all, is the one when my Grandmother Webster was present. She and her sons, my uncles, Henry, Andrew and Colin came in a sleigh, arriving about dusk on a clear, cold Christmas day. My mother had been cooking, baking and cleaning for some time. We had a wonderful feast of fresh fowl and all the trimmings as well as the traditional plum pudding with lemon sauce, shortbread and fruit cakes.

We stood and sang the Doxology before we sat down, my father at the head of the table, mother opposite.

It was a happy evening. My Uncle Colin tuned his violin, my Uncle Henry played a piccolo, and Mother sang. The tunes were all the old, well-loved Scottish songs. The violin alone squeaked out the reels and strathspeys. My uncle was not a professional, but I loved it. Then came the specialty! Uncle Andrew, his mother's darling, danced the Highland Fling beautifully and authentically. Later he taught it to me. He finished with something we had never seen before, the sword dance. In lieu of swords, he put two pieces of wood crosswise on the floor. As Colin played, Andrew pirouetted with his pointed toes around, about and between those crossed sticks, never touching one of them. I can imagine how he would have looked with a kilt flying. It was beautiful.

All this and their talk about books and music and the football [soccer] scores in Glasgow seemed incongruous on the prairie, when I now recall it.

At that time, they had been fifteen years away from their home in Port Glasgow where they had been born and raised until misfortune came upon them. As a result, my grandparents emigrated to Canada with their adult children.

My Grandfather Webster had been a successful merchant in Port Glasgow, a small town a short distance from Glasgow, and a shipping port on the river Clyde. History tells of the financial crisis which happened to Britain at the end of the nineteenth century. This family, like many others, had lived in luxury.

My aunts and uncles, in addition to attending school, had violin, piano and dancing lessons. My mother attended a finishing school where she studied piano, voice and elocution, learned how to sew a fine seam, and was instructed in all the social graces necessary for a young woman of her class. Poor training for a pioneer wife.

How and why they found themselves in the far west is another story.

Editors' Note. That the memory of music plays an important part in this story, speaks to Janet's future life; music became a part of who she was.

Classical music was her first choice, followed closely by the contents of the Presbyterian Hymnal. Pop tunes could also be found in her house, and often a score from a popular Broadway show was on the piano. Janet had no formal musical training, but did possess a nice soprano voice. She married a man who felt about music as did she. Malcolm was a tenor with near perfect pitch, (which drove him to distraction, on occasion, when one of his children was practicing voice) and before arthritis crippled his hands, many a gathering saw him take down his violin, "the fiddle" and, usually playing with a friend or two, fill the house with Scottish tunes, and other melodies they knew by heart.

For her children, musical training was almost a necessity; all eight, at one time or another, had music lesson. All from an early age sang in church and/or school choirs and played in orchestras and bands. One of her children was a Metropolitan Opera Regional Semi-Finalist, and another sang for years in an auditioned civic choir. They played instruments as varied as the violin, tuba and glockenspiel. Two children were music majors in college and had careers in the field. But nothing brought her as much pleasure as seeing them all gathered around the piano, in the big white house on Common Road, or in later years, in one of her children's homes. One would be at the piano, accompanying; perhaps one would be playing the guitar; and all would be singing. Memories of those musical family gatherings on the prairie must have echoed in her heart.

Janet's Uncle Henry; Janet's mother, Elizabeth; and Janet's Aunt Phemie Webster. Stranraer, Scotland, 1858.

Elizabeth McLeod Webster Ross,
Janet's mother, Greenock, Scotland, 1885.

THE NEIGHBORS ON THIRTY-FOUR

By the year 1900 our school district, and Kinbrae school district, due south of Clumber, were beginning to be populated. Homesteaders drifted in from Germany, all the Scandinavian countries and, of course, Ireland, England and Scotland. Americans came, too. Their parents had pioneered in the Dakotas, Wisconsin and Minnesota. They were better equipped and more knowledgeable about farming and showed real progress at an earlier date.

The most interesting and intriguing family were the Baughs. I don't know what year they came, but it seemed they had always been across the Cut Arm Creek, in a roomy house built of stone. That home was a castle to me. The window sills were two feet deep. It stood, chalet fashion, on the side of a steep bank. The east wall faced the creek and meadow below.

The large parlor and kitchen were on the first floor. A flight of stairs led to the sleeping quarters which were partly nestled in a bank. One more flight led to an airy bright chamber equipped as an office and sewing room combined. From there, you could step out and walk along the bank.

We knew them as good neighbors and sometimes, as a family, we were invited to visit them. At those times Mr. Baugh and my mother would sing duets. He had a beautiful tenor voice and I liked to listen. My ears picked up some laughter and negative remarks about the new love songs from the sheet music their daughters owned. I noticed they sang them, however. Grace, the oldest daughter, played the piano very well.

Mr. Baugh never appeared to farm much. He mostly had a hired man. He did work with his beautiful horses and was known as a horse trader. From whence did he get the wherewith-all to provide so much luxury for his family, in a country so recently abandoned by the native people?

It was no secret. Mr. Baugh was a remittance man. When one found out his full name, of which his six children were very proud, it was easily deduced the family in England was paying to keep him in Canada.

Charles Spencer Winston Churchill Baugh was from a family of class and power. That he was addicted to alcohol was no secret. One man told this story: "When I first met Charley Baugh, he was down on all fours on the creek bank howling like a wolf."

Mrs. Baugh, dear lady, was the first person my father ploughed his team through the snow to fetch, to assist at my entrance to the chilly world.

Mrs. Baugh did not ever have much to say. Although my mother visited with her, she was somewhat of an enigma. There were many rumors that apart from his drinking, Charlie had seduced, then married the Irish maid. Indeed, she was Irish and had a kind heart. "God bless her."

Their eldest son, Hume, was sent to Toronto where ultimately, he became a Doctor of Medicine. Grace became a teacher and married late. Hattie married a neighbor farm boy. (How I admired her at the fairs astride a beautifully groomed saddle horse, dressed in the full cowgirl regalia of that day.)

Charlie, the younger son, died in the First World War the day the Armistice was signed

I have taken pleasure in remembering these neighbors from my youth, the Baughs.

TRAINS

In the nostalgic trips I have been taking through my early life, my acquaintance with trains and their importance at that time must not be neglected.

Trains! I loved them. I love them still. Sometimes I long to hear their mournful whistle and distant rumble in the dead of night, or any other time. It's probably because the train was so important to me personally. We lived six miles straight south of the town where the railroad station stood.

When I left home in 1916 to live in Winnipeg with my cousins and attend the Collegiate Institute, I took the train. When I went to teach in a slightly remote district, too far to drive, what else? I took the train.

That sounds easy, but thinking about it tells me it was not. My father or my brother had to harness the horses and hitch them to the vehicles at a very early hour. That train went west stopping in Bredenbury promptly at eight in the morning every day, and east at six o'clock every evening. You were there promptly or you had to wait twenty-four hours to make your journey.

The particular morning about which I write, was cold,

very cold. I dressed in my warmest clothes. My brother brought the team and sleigh to the door. My father pulled a stone, a little larger than a football, out of the oven, wrapped it in some cloth, put it in the sleigh under my feet, and threw a horse blanket about my shoulders.

My brother started the team and we were off. He stood in his ancient buffalo overcoat with his back turned partly to the north wind, glancing sidewise once in a while to keep an eye on the team. The going was slow. It had snowed for a couple of days and the trail had not been broken. It was up to Bob and Peary to plow through. We knew we might be late so my brother urged the horses on.

When we came to the town and turned right onto the main street, the train was at the station coughing, belching clouds of steam. The team seemed to sense an urgency and took off at a gallop. We flew down that stretch of street. I picked up my suitcase and ran up the stairs of the station platform just as the train started to move! Too late! Then, it stopped among clouds of steam. I jumped on the steps, the conductor grabbed my bag, shut the door and with a lurch we went forward.

I took all that in stride until later when my brother told me, "Do you realize that the engineer stopped the train for you"?

It was a sobering incident. Everyone knew trains did not stop for anything. The Canadian Pacific Railroad train had stopped for me, a youthful country schoolmarm. I am thankful to this day. I have also learned to have gratitude to my parents and brother who worked so hard to get me to that platform, something I took for granted at the time.

MY FIRST TEACHING EXPERIENCE

KINBRAE

1917

The winter of nineteen seventeen brought realization that Kaiser Wilhelm and his war machine was not, definitely not, going to be easily beaten.

War fever was high all over the Dominion of Canada. It infected every area of life. The Winnipeg Collegiate Institute where I was a student was no exception.

In one of my classes a young man, Walter Yarrow, represented the Y.M.C.A. in their war effort. He ran an "Earn and Give" campaign. His salesmanship and powers of persuasion led us to believe that in summer vacation anyone of us could earn at least ten dollars.

That was well and good for city folks. Giving no thought of how or where I could earn anything at all in my Saskatchewan prairie home, I blithely signed my name to a note promising I would earn and give that amount in the coming summer.

It was good to be home. The sultry summer days were lovely. The high cerulean blue sky, brilliant at night with stars, cradling never ending fleecy clouds by day, the wheat fields, sloughs, and poplar woods were there to love and enjoy. The city, school and war seemed very far away.

I did what I could to help my mother with the same old women's work that never ended. It was fun to be with my two younger sisters and my littlest brother was always a pleasure.

The first letter from Walter Yarrow demanding the ten dollars, as we would say today, "shook me up" and gave me something about which to worry.

One afternoon alone in the house I answered our phone. Two longs and one short ring meant the Ross house. A man's voice asked for Miss Ross. "This is Miss Ross". That was the way I had been addressed all year by the teachers so that response came naturally. The voice answered quite banteringly, "So you're Miss Ross now?". I quickly, ungently, hung the receiver on its cradle as my mother entered. I was scolded quite firmly for being so impolite to anyone who phoned our house. No use trying to explain that whomever it had been was rude and, I thought, belittling to me.

Our ring again. This time the voice became George Hook, a neighbor and the Board President of the Kinbrae School District south of us. This time he was not teasing, but asked, almost begged me to teach in the school for two weeks. The contracted teacher could not be there and the district would lose their government grant if the school did not open on time. I was glad to accept even though he thought this little girl he had known all her life was "giving herself airs".

The days flew by until the school was to open. I fantasized my role as a teacher and tried to remember all the necessary procedures I observed as a student over the years. So, it was I had no qualms about my ability to handle the job for such a short time.

My misgivings began when my father announced that Bob and the cart would be my mode of transportation. That cart! Good grief! It had only two wheels and axle with a carriage, a seat and a dashboard. It had been purchased, not for racing, but for my younger sisters to drive themselves to school. Two wheels could not cramp and turn the vehicle over as could happen to a buggy if the horse shied and turned quickly. The cart may have been safe but to my teenage eyes it was a monstrosity.

The morning had come. The cart with Bob was at the door. I had nothing to do but climb into the despised contraption and sit on the seat which seemed too far from the ground to be safe. Dad handed me up the reigns saying "Be careful", and slapped Bob gently on the hip. "Getup!" We were off! The beautiful morning, I could not enjoy. I was no horse person and being so close to the bronco's rump made me quake. We did arrive after four long miles of rutted prairie trail, some proper road and a bridge across the creek.

Now to unhitch Bob, lead him to the barn, tie him to the stall and remove his bridle. That was a law. You did not permit a horse to stand for long with a bit in his mouth. I knew Bob had a reputation for being improperly broken and was very squeamish of anyone touching his ears.

As I gingerly put my hand on the top of his head to grab the bridle, he instantly flew back till he was nearly on his haunches with the halter rope taut. When I moved away, he relaxed. This went on at least three times until I had won. Every day, morning and afternoon, the same thing happened.

I think he knew I was afraid of him and when he rolled those white eyes my way, I was.

School was much easier. I was not afraid to stand before the group of children differing in age from seven to thirteen or fourteen. They numbered below twenty and all were well behaved. The grade levels were sorted out and worn text books put to use.

It took very little time for me to notice during the lunch and recess breaks that there was something amiss in the students' games. Three of them were always left out, ignored, or meanly treated by all the others. I knew by their language that they were of foreign parentage and, on looking it up, found the name Ludke. The family had immigrated from Germany just before World War One began. Those children were German and being punished for something in which they had no part. Endeavoring to include them, I talked to them at recess. I called on them for responses in all their classes and reprimanded anyone who made derogatory remarks to them. Months later Mrs. Ludke met my mother by chance in town and told her she wished I had stayed as their teacher because I was kind to her children.

That is not quite the end of the story. There was a matter of renumeration. In two or three weeks I received a check in the mail for the colossal sum of ten dollars. I never did see George Hook. Maybe he was ashamed of paying me so little.

That ten dollars was very welcome. I could now pay off my promissory note and receive no more nasty reminders from Mr. Yarrow. My dad teased me for a long time about being talked into a promise I was not sure I could fulfill. In that area I might just be a slow learner to this day.

A MOTHER'S DILEMMA

This little incident is a poignant memory of the First World War.

In the summer of nineteen sixteen, I was home from school in Winnipeg and very happy. My oldest brother, Alex, was also home on his last furlough before going overseas. The farm was running smoothly and my father was glad of the extra help from this son who had enlisted in The Canadian Armed Forces just over a year ago.

War fever was very high in Canada at the time. Patriotic Britishers knew they had to do their bit. That Kaiser Bill would get his comeuppance! This war would not last another year. And so, the young men, or should I say not quite men, of the prairies in all their naivete and innocence, rallied to the call. How little they could even imagine what lay ahead. All they knew or felt was pride, pride in being young and strong and in uniform. And above all pride in doing their duty. Duty, where has that word gone? We hardly hear it anymore, but I digress.

All six children were home for the last time, but of that we had no premonition.

Forbes, the youngest, that "come late" baby I have mentioned, was barely two and still nursing, which sometimes gave our mum a problem. I don't believe she had the courage to listen to his howling protests if she told him, "You are a big boy now, drink from a cup".

The time came in late August when Alex's furlough was over. The troop train he had to board would be running on Canadian National Railway tracks. The closest railroad station on the track was twenty-five miles away and the train would be passing through sometime in the night.

About three o'clock on the appointed day, we gathered around our hero brother. It was a lovely sunshiny day with a hint of autumn in the air. But there was gloomy autumn in our collective mood. Mum admonished us about caring for Forbes and very anxiously left him in our keeping. Her oldest son, our hero, helped her to the front seat of the buckboard, slung his duffle bag aboard and stepped up to the back seat. My father flipped the reigns at the horses and we all said "Good bye".

It was not until then that I broke into copious tears.

I do not remember much about the evening except that it was about three o'clock in the morning when our parents returned.

At a late breakfast we learned they had suffered a very unpleasant time.

It was past six and darkness had almost fallen before they reached the railroad station. There was no town, no restaurant.

The station was bleak and empty, only dimly lighted. The Master, Bob Gray, was getting ready to close up and go home. There would be no more scheduled trains that night. When the troop train would arrive, he did not know and if Alex was to board the speeding, smokey monster it would have to be signaled to stop. I think Mr. Gray set up the signals necessary and invited the three Rosses, my parents and my brother, to his home. His wife, Lois, was the daughter of the Clumber District Post Master.

It seemed only natural that they expected to be given food at the supper hour. Sharing with visitors was the custom in western hospitality and they needed food. Lois welcomed them to her bare little home, but there were no signs of something to eat. After visiting for a while, Alex became restless and suggested he had better get back to the station. He dare not miss that train. It was then Lois went to the kitchen and came back with tea in china cups and some dainty sandwiches on a plate. Mother and son each took one sandwich and when the plate was passed to Dad, he accepted the plate and ate the remaining sandwiches. All he could say in self-defense was, "I wasn't paying attention. I thought she had given everyone a plate and that was mine". He had been talking with Mr. Gray.

Along with Mr. Gray, they went back to the station and began their vigil. Mother told us, "I was torn between my wee son and my big one". There lay the darling of her heart, his six foot two stretched out on a wooden railroad bench asleep, his duffle bag under his head. She worried. Those rough army puttees must be uncomfortable. What was happening back home? Did her little boy cry for her? Did he go to sleep? Were the older children patient? On and on her anxieties grew.

Hours dragged by, as they say, morosely. In the dim light, they watched the apple of their eyes, in rough private's uniform, sleep the sleep of childhood.

At last what did they hear, a faint whistle? A rumble? The train was coming. Quickly they roused their sleeping son and were on the dark platform in the glaring engine light.

The thing stopped, a door opened, Alex leaped up the steps, duffle bag on his shoulder. The door slammed. One more flower of the West plucked for the carnage of Europe.

He was killed at Vimy Ridge, May 1917. The lad had become a Sergeant leading his company in a reconnoitering objective between the lines.

The letter said he had volunteered.

Editors' Note. Twenty-five years later, almost to the month her brother John Alexander left for World War One, Janet faced a similar mother's dilemma. Her oldest son was to return to the army after his furlough, and she herself was awaiting the eminent birth of a "come late" baby. The day he was to leave, she knew the baby was coming-soon. What to do? Stay home and try to be comfortable, or go with Malcolm and spend a few precious moments more with her son? She got into the car and went to wave him off to war. Twelve hours later the baby was born. This time, the John Alexander to whom she bid farewell returned safely from World War Two.

John Alexander Ross, Janet's brother, killed in the battle for Vimy Ridge in World War One, May 1917.

Elizabeth Ross, wearing the Memorial Cross
presented to her by the Prince of Wales in honor
of her son who died in World War One.

POETRY

SPRING 1945

I hung my wash on the line today
Beside the maple trees,
And the khaki shirts reached out and danced
With the Navy dungarees.

The spring breeze played a merry tune
As it rustled the tender leaves,
And my heart sang a joyful song
As glad as the wind in the trees.

For hadn't my soldier come home
From the war,
And my sailor from the seas.

Editors' Note. Written after Janet and Malcolm's sons returned safely from World War II.

PRAIRIE CHILD

God, I have loved your world
Since I found the pale anemones
Between flat rocks
In the tender grass
Cropped short by cows,
And sat on a smooth stone
Warmed by your sun
And felt enwrapped by love
And Life.
I knew you were there.

How else could a little child with
Tangled hair
And pale from winter's long imprisonment
feel the pulse of spring
and know that you are good,
And raise in childish treble
A wordless song of Joy?

I knew that you were good.

JUNE

So, this is June?
Cold, damp, quiet.
Give me back my other Junes;
Hot, hectic happy.

Graduation days synonymous with June and June bugs;
Big, clumsy, flying hither and yon
Crashing against every lighted window.

It is that happy time and it is too warm.
Filmy dresses wilt before the party is over.
Brand new suits show signs of moisture
But the celebrating goes on.

Joy of accomplishment, pride of success.
Freedom from study, at least for a little while.
And dreams, dreams of adult life to come.

Youth, beautiful youth!
Who would not hover near them and enjoy?

CHRISTMAS AFTERMATH

The pots and pans are neatly stacked,
The kitchen back to normal,
Each knife and spoon in its normal place,
Neat, quiet.

The birds gorged all week long
On crumbs from our Christmas feasting,
Ruffled feathers and twittered thanks
'Til the sun went down,
Dark, quiet.

All week our souls have feasted
On giving, taking, loving, laughing.
The Christmas week was bright.
We waved the last car away today
Together, quiet.

LOOKING BACK

Oh, we have seen a golden sea,
Great miles of waving grain,
In another land in other years
On a fertile, pregnant plain.

And as we thrilled to its beauty,
And its richness held in store,
Little we dreamed of another sea
On a distant southern shore.
There we someday would wander
On the lovely silver sand,
And joy in the voice of the ocean
As it laughs and licks the sand.

We ponder all the secrets
Hid in its cavernous deep,
And we thank our God for the years we had
For a lifetime to laugh and weep.

Editors' Note. After retirement, Janet and Malcolm spent many winters in Florida, where this poem was written.

A HAPPENING

Mary, you have lived the moment, promised for all
Time....

The instant came- surcease from pain.
You felt his warm, moist body brush your flesh.
You heard his cry and heaved a deep long sigh
and then.... content.

Relaxed, the tears traced down your temple
Dampening your tangled hair.
Did you whisper "Messiah?" "Immanuel?"
"Christ is born?"

Mary, did Joseph caress your brow, and in awe
And consternation did your souls cry out
"What now.... what now?"

PLANTING

We put each bulb down in its place
And smoothed the worked-up sod
Your little friend asked, "What you doin'?"
You said, "I'm helping God".

The kindergarten skeptic asked,
"You are? Well where is He?"
Your answer, "All around the world.
He is here with you and me.

He made the world so beautiful
We try to keep it so
By planting pretty flowers
And helping them to grow."

Now you are making beauty
In a very different way.
You travel to your city school
On every kind of day.
Your students know you will be there
With courage and good grace.
The challenge of a new day
You see on every face.

You no longer help with tulips
Or plant things in the sod
But in your classroom situation
You are planting and helping God.

Editors' Note. This is based on an actual story; The child who gave the above answer to a friend, found a vocation teaching for many years in a city school district.

THE GARBAGE MAN

I like to watch from the window
To see the garbage man.
Who comes around in his big truck
To empty our shining can.

When I call and wave my hand
He waves back at me.
I really think our garbage man
Is pleasant as can be.

When I am big, I want to drive
A great big garbage truck.
And go to all the houses
To pick the garbage up.

If someday a little boy
Waves his hand at me,
I'll wave my hand right back at him
As pleased as I can be.

Editors' Note: Written for a grandchild who loved big trucks.

LISTEN

There are little boys around the world
Who love to run and play,
And very, very often
They have things to say.

Sometimes people listen,
And sometimes they do not,
But they just keep on speaking
Because they think a lot.

My grandson always speaks to me,
And I listen to every word,
Because he wants to talk about
The things he's seen and heard.

And things always seem wonderful
And bright and full of joy,
So I am very happy
That I have this little boy.

TO A CHRISTMAS CACTUS

Such a tiny Christmas Cactus!
Every day I pass you by
And wonder why they left you there
Unwatered, pale and dry.

Then they put you around the corner
In an inconspicuous nook.
A short time before Christmas
I thought I'd take a look.

On every once-sad stem,
A lovely blossom grew.
And then I looked more closely
To see if it was you.

Christmas choirs are singing, and loud is every bell,
Telling about the Christ child, but they do not do as well
As the vision of hope and love and
promise that you have given me,
By your sudden burst of beauty
Dear little Cactus Tree.

Editors' Note. This poem was written the last Christmas of Janet's life.

STORIES ABOUT MY FATHER

THE ROSS FAMILY AND JAMES JOHN (JACK) ROSS

Editors' Note. Although never completed, Janet intended to write fully about the Ross family, her father's family. To that end, she kept notes and sketches. Repetitious at times, we have decided to include them, slightly condensed, in their entirety because her writing is beautiful and because, taken together, they provide background for her Prairie Stories.

STORY ONE

My Grandfather Ross was gray haired and bearded when he and his eldest son, William, decided that the motherless family now had outgrown the land their family had occupied for generations, a small farm near Lord Dalrymple's estate. According to historical records found in the library at Stranraer, Scotland, John Ross also worked, part time, on the Estate.

My uncle Will went to Africa and worked in the diamond mines until he earned enough money to take the entire family, six in all, to what they thought would be Manitoba a western province in Canada. I heard my father say that his father planned and talked for years of going to Man-i-to-BA as he pronounced it. There must have been a great deal of government promotion and emphasis on the benefits of emigrating to Manitoba.

In any case, my Uncle returned from the Gold Coast with the means to book comfortable passage for the entire family.

An incident which may have embittered my father occurred shortly before they left Scotland. Uncle Will decided to marry his sweetheart, Bessie, and take her along. Since there was no passage provided for her, the youngest son was relegated to the only place available, in steerage. He never mentioned this to us children, but I was told by my mother, secretly. Poor Dad! What a blow to his pride, as class consciousness was still strong.

STORY TWO

John Ross and his family left Port Logan near the Estate of Lord Dalrymple near Stranraer, Scotland, where the family had farmed for generations.

They booked passage in the spring of 1883 for Canada, destination, Manitoba.

After a long sea voyage which terminated at the port of Montreal they traveled by rail as far as the Canadian Pacific Railroad was finished. Then by oxcart they set out to find a suitable place to homestead.

The father liked the terrain on the banks of the Cut Arm Creek and stopped there not knowing they had over reached the western border of Manitoba.

There were no white settlers in the area. The Rosses were the first. In that lonely wilderness they found some narrow place in the Creek. When other settlers arrived, they called it Ross's Crossing. For many years the bridge that was eventually constructed there was known by that name.

William and John chose the Eastern Quarters of Section 2; Range 1, West of 2nd Meridian as their homesteads. On Will's quarter they built a house of the plentiful and available poplar logs. When William had completed his resident requirement on his homestead, Bessie, expecting her first child, persuaded him to go to Winnipeg. There he set up a coal and wood business which he ran until nineteen sixteen.

The aging father went with them, as did daughters Annie and Maggie. He died at age ninety. Mary, another daughter, married Peter Gunn of Perley who became a highly respected farmer, well-known in Saltcoats.

STORY THREE

My grandfather, John Ross had long dreamed and hoped to be able to go to Manitoba in the new world. For years the British had been hyping this Colony as a veritable land of promise. How to transport a family of six there was beyond the means of anything he could save or earn.

It was unthinkable for his daughters to go into service. Although they kept care of their own home and cared for the younger children, they had servants, milk-maids and washer-women, who took care of the menial tasks their station in life would not allow them to do.

There were opportunities to earn money in other areas of the Empire, especially Africa where the diamond mines were flourishing.

William, the oldest son, departed thither and in due time returned to London. There he booked passage to Canada for the whole family.

The spring of 1883 found them in Montreal from where they took a Canadian Pacific train as far west as the rails were laid, to Winnipeg, Manitoba.

From there they traveled in caravans of ox drawn Red River Carts and covered wagons.

In the middle of the twentieth century the ruts from the many heavy wheels remained along the Qu'Appelle Valley banks. They were also discernible on the North bank of our Cut Arm Creek.

About two hundred miles from Winnipeg, the family left the caravan. That area was gouged out by ravines and not to my grandfather's liking. They would have to cross the creek. On the other side, the bank was smoother, if steeper, ending abruptly in the broad level prairie. The wide creek banks, the meadow and the stream with its vegetation had sufficient beauty to suffice the elder Ross. He chose the location for their homesteads.

To cross the creek, there was no semblance of a bridge. The men searched for the narrowest place in the stream. The women, high up in the Red River Cart, were pulled across the water by the goaded oxen. No white woman had ever forded that creek before. Future maps were to call it Ross's Crossing.

There are books published in Canada telling something of the brave and hardy people who began to settle the west at that time. I have no knowledge of how they were temporarily housed or how they managed; one family alone in that vast wilderness.

A respectable log house was built on Uncle Will's quarter where all lived until Bessie, his new wife, became terrified of bearing her first child in such primitive conditions

Since he had been in possession of his homestead sufficient time to satisfy government requirements, and had a building, also required, Uncle Will could leave. The whole family of women, and my grandfather retreated to Winnipeg. There William's first son was born, Percy John, who always felt his mother cheated him out to the distinction of being the first white child born in that area of the North West Territories.

My father, James John, or Jack as he was called, remained and occupied the house until he and mother married and had two sons, Alexander and Colin. They moved onto our own quarter, South East Quarter of Section 2, West of 2nd Meridian where I was born, in 1901.

One of my father's sisters, Mary, married another homesteader, Peter Gunn, and stayed in the Perley area. The other sisters married in Winnipeg and none ever visited the prairie again.

That left Jack, my father, alone to eke out a living. No one in this generation, I am sure, can even imagine what toil, sacrifices, and disappointments the emigrants endured. Among them all, the loneliness was indeed the most painful. Those who endured deserve much credit.

STORY FOUR

I have told many times of the family of John Ross, a man with snow white beard and hair to match, emigrating to Canada with four daughters, Janet, Mary, Annie and Maggie, and two sons William and James John and a daughter in law, Bessie. His wife had died in the youngest's infancy.

My father James John, Jack as he was called, was the second youngest, twenty years old when they emigrated from Scotland.

They made friends with the Indians which was an asset in later years. Not so the timber wolves and bears.

Dad was left alone when the family returned to Winnipeg.

Bits and pieces of happenings over the next ten years add flavor to his story.

He went to the "States" to get work on the railroad and would have probably been able to save a nice nest egg to use on his homestead. However, to work on the railroad, it was mandatory that he become an American citizen. It speaks to his Britishness that he told the story. "When it came to the part where I had to swear allegiance to the U.S. and renounce all loyalties, especially to Queen Victoria, I put my hand down and walked out". He went back to what, I do not know. Pure loneliness. By 1890 some more settlers were beginning to arrive and in 1893 the Websters, my mother's family, came and were shortly his neighbors.

During the North-West Rebellion of 1885 often called the Riel Rebellion, he decided to enlist in the North-West Field Force. So, after walking one hundred miles to Regina and being sworn in, he was promptly put on guard duty. Fortunately, the Indians and their leader Louis Riel, soon gave up and his feet were spared.

STORY FIVE

This effort is an exercise in memory. Over the years, inklings of incidents in my father, Jack Ross's life seemed notable to me. Here are a few.

This is about his education, in Scotland. The school was an all boy institution as was the custom of the times.

The master, as he was called, ruled with a hickory rod. As each apprehensive boy lined up behind another at the entrance, no one knew who would receive a sharp blow from the rod. They knew someone would or more than one. "Spare the rod and spoil the child", was this master's adage.

Each child took his turn in carrying a 'chunk' of peat for the fire. That seemed crude to us [children on the prairie in Saskatchewan] whose school was supplied with firewood by the school board.

Whatever the circumstances, Jack did learn to "read, write and cipher", also Euclid. (He was proud when I studied geometry.) There was also Latin, but what he remembered of that is questionable. "Amo, amas, amat" was all I remember him repeating.

As for his religious education, all he had to say was that in Scotland, his father and the complete family walked five miles to church every Sunday. However, he could and did recite the shorter catechism and snatches of the old Scottish Psalter. I am still thankful for that. He knew plenty of Proverbs and passages from Ecclesiastes. Some examples are: "Pride goeth before a fall and a haughty spirit before destruction." Or "The fool goes back to his folly like a dog to his vomit." "The fool and his money are soon parted" and "The way of the transgressor is hard, and unhappy is he who walketh therein".

Editors' Note. In spite of the harsh circumstance of his education, mother would often repeat to us what she heard him say over and over, "Education is an easy thing to carry". She believed this as fervently as did he.

STORY SIX

In early days my father lived as a bachelor homesteader. A diversion he enjoyed was attending evangelistic meetings. It seems there were no shortage of traveling preachers. As in Lincoln's time, they roamed the prairie. When a tent meeting was held, settlers came from miles around. In the early days, that was their opportunity to gather and socialize as well as sing, listen and pray.

Bachelors like my father must have loved those breaks in monotony. It was not all solemnity; plenty of pranks were played on each other.

As a result, a benefit I indirectly received is a familiarity with the tunes and verses from those 'old rouser' hymns, which some denominations still use. He did not pretend to teach us but we heard them often as he hummed snatches while doing his chores.

That Jack Ross loved the beauty of nature there was no doubt. He cherished every tree though they were only poplars. His admonition "never destroy a tree" is still with me. Every evening near sunset, he walked to the valley bank, where he stood and watched the stars appear one by one. As dark began to fall he came back with remarks such as: "it's a beautiful evening", "the wind is changing", "if the wind goes down tonight, we will have frost." If the wheat was still in the early stages of growth, that projected another failed crop and all the consequences.

STORY SEVEN

A little history.

Children do not often listen carefully to tales told or remarks made about their parents' early lives or ancestral history. It was common knowledge among the cousins that there were explorers in the Ross family, many years before. In fact, we could find on the map of the arctic circle the Ross River flowing into the MacKenzie River, which flowed to the Arctic Ocean. We were not impressed.

We knew our Grandfather Ross was interested in navigation. Some of his heavy books along with his Bible were still in existence when we were young. He had been studying them (about navigation) until he was ninety years of age. We children on the prairie thought that was ridiculous. Little we knew that the sea was in his blood. If there were no other means of the livelihood for the strong young yeoman of the era, they could always "go to the sea". The British Navy in her heyday of strength could certainly use them, and she did.

In his book, "The Arctic Grail", 1988, Canadian author Pierre Berton tells of Commander John Ross and his three decades of sea experience. Ross was brave and he had been wounded thirteen times in battle. He and his nephew James Clark Ross spent four years in the arctic gaining valuable information. Both men were knighted for their contributions to the Empire.

Farley Mowat's "Ordeal on Ice" is a lesser volume containing pertinent information and is obtainable in most libraries.

These books are exciting and informative for anyone interested in that aspect of the human experience. They are to me, concrete evidence that my famous relatives did exist.

THE McLEOD HERITAGE

THE McLEOD HERITAGE

Forward
By Janet Ross McLeod
1989

I have written this essay in the interest of my deceased husband, Malcolm McLeod's, and my grandchildren, who have expressed a wish to know more of their ancestors.

I shall strive to record some of what I have been told by him and have observed during contact with his family.

Anything I have written about the Clan MacLeod history has been taken from the booklet of that name written by I.F Grant, from Johnstone's Clan History.

Janet McLeod

From earliest times, the inhabitants of Scotland's Western Isles, who claimed Norse decent, were divided into clans. Their common language was Gaelic, to which they clung despite invasions by Norsemen, Romans, Angles or Normans.

The history of the MacLeod clan is one of the most interesting and important of all the clan stories.

The Norsemen were absorbed into Gaeldom in the twelfth or thirteenth centuries. It was in this circa that Leod, who founded the clan, appeared and flourished. According to tradition, he was descended from the Royal House of Norway. A point of interest, there was a King Alexander and a Chief Malcolm who reigned in ancient Norway.

During the course of history, two MacLeod clans emerged, friendly at first, but later feuding. One clan occupied the Southern Islands and the other occupied the largest and most Northerly of the Hebrides chain, the Island of Lewis and Harris.

It is said that as late as the sixteenth century, this clan retained some of the Druid myths, superstitions, and belief in fairies. The stones of Callanish, which are similar to the ones at Stonehenge, in England, were believed to be part of the Druid form of worship.

The Lewis end of the Island of Lewis and Harris, is a stark and somewhat barren land. The rockbound and rugged coasts are pounded by waves and winds off the North Atlantic.

The country people lived on tracts of farm land called Crofts. Many of them still do. Their crops were mainly oats, and vegetables. Fish were plentiful.

The main crop was, and still is, wool. Thousands of sheep graze on vast stretches of green and rocky land. The landscape and seascapes are very lovely.

For many centuries the wool was produced on looms in the homes of the crofters. It was washed, carded, spun, dyed and woven into cloth called tweed, which is still manufactured and highly prized today. It was also made into the colorful tartans, or plaids which identify the highland clans. The yellow and black belongs to the MacLeods of Lewis and is the tartan Malcolm McLeod, the son of Allan MacLeod, who was born on Lewis, wore, and which his children and grandchildren continue to wear.

Gaelic, Malcolm's first language, was and is their native tongue. They were a proud people, independent, sensitive, intelligent, mostly deeply religious and knowledgeable in many areas. Most could read at least the Bible and nearly all were devoted to the Church of Scotland.

Artisans and craftsmen flourished in the cities. The nineteenth century produced economists, psychologists and students of divinity, as well as doctors and other professionals.

History tells that the MacLeod clan was famous for its musical ability. Love of music and bagpipes is evidenced in the MacLeod branch of Vancouver, British Columbia, Canada. John Angus MacLeod, son of Malcolm's brother, John Murdo MacLeod, won a medal, in the 1970's, in pibroch piping at The Royal Edinburgh Military Tattoo. A Canadian, he was the first piper not born in Scotland to do so. The Michigan McLeods also have accomplished musicians.

During the latter half of the nineteenth century, the

British Government, in the interests of Colonization and concern for the over population of the Northern Islands, devised a plan to persuade and meagerly assist any who were brave enough to emigrate to that great Northwestern plain, known then as the North West Territories, which eventually became Saskatchewan, Canada. The emigration of Allan and Mary MacLeod was a result of the above, and not because of the Clearances forced upon the Islanders from about 1750-1860

Allan MacLeod was born outside of Stornoway, the capital of Lewis and Harris, on Croft Number 17, Col, Back in 1860. He died in Saltcoats, SK, Canada, in 1939. His wife, Mary Stewart, was born in 1865 in Scotland and died in Saltcoats, SK 1943.

Allan and Mary, with their two small children, Isabelle and Jean and another one expected, were among those who sailed to Canada about July, 1888. It was a very uncomfortable journey lasting twenty-seven days.

Many were ill and the oxen in the hold did not add to the comfort.

Arrival at Riverside, near Dunrae, Manitoba brought to an end their promised enticement to adventure. From there on, they were on their own. Each family head was given a quarter section, 160 acres, of land, a plow, a team of oxen and, I have heard from another source, ten dollars.

They managed somehow. Who knows? I might insert here, Allan MacLeod was a stonemason, no mean trade, and certainly would be in demand on that particular area of prairie, as there were plenty of stones and no houses. In the town of Saltcoats, where he later moved, he built a church sanctuary that is used today. The congregation is celebrating its one hundred birthday this year. Also, a stone firewall of like vintage still stands. (Editors' Note. A wall that was built by Allan also still stands on the Isle of Lewis and Harris.)

They stayed in Dunrae until 1901 and Angus, Neil, Maggie and Malcolm were born, and also two other children who died as infants and who are buried there.

It seems appropriate at this time to explain that Malcolm was independent at an early age. When signing documents for the purchase of some land he hoped to own, he chose to use the "Mc" instead of the "Mac" spelling in his name. This may have pained his father and it has given some of his offspring a pain to explain.

According to the Encyclopedia Britannica, "Mac", "Mc", or "M", prefixing a name, all mean "son of". So, MacLeod or McLeod both mean the same and Leod is pronounced loud.

They again settled near another Stornoway, farther west, this time in Saskatchewan, in a Gaelic speaking community. Gaelic was the only language spoken in the Allan MacLeod home, and it was Malcolm's first language, the one he spoke exclusively until he started school. There they remained and raised eleven children, four more, Allan, John, Donald and Stewart being born in Saskatchewan.

The father, Allan, grew the best potatoes in that countryside. In the winter he brought home frozen fish from the frozen lakes to supplement the diet of beef and pork.

Mary, the mother, provided barley and oat cakes and tender scones baked on top the of the stove. A dozen loaves of bread were baked twice a week and all grew strong and healthy.

One of Allan's first endeavors was to see that a house of worship was built. This being accomplished with all speed, a minister was called.

The congregation, mostly a group of reformers in the oldest and strictest traditions of the Church of Scotland, allowed no musical instrument. There was psalm singing as in the Hebrew form of worship. A cantor began the song by singing the first bars of the tune, the people joining in and following his leadership. With his beautiful tenor voice and perfect pitch, Allan was the main cantor for the congregation.

Mary also had a splendid voice and added much to the church service. For many years this practice continued in the Gaelic tongue.

It was not until the second generation, who spoke English, came along that an organ was purchased. Then there were two services, one in each language. Allan continued as Cantor as long as he was able.

Among other things that were known about this gentle man was his compassionate care for all members of the Gaelic speaking settlement. Anytime help was needed, he would go to homes of illness and grief. He was called to assist at births when no doctor was available. Often, he took the place of a mortician. When the 1918 influenza epidemic struck, he was not afraid to help care for the sick or dying, never becoming ill himself. Often, he officiated at funerals, reading the Bible and praying.

With his own family he was strict but respected. There were prayers at every meal and every evening the father read passages from the Bible. All of them knelt by their chairs as he said prayers. This was a custom in many Scottish homes for generations.

The door of his home was always open to strangers and friends alike. Homeless men were sheltered there some winters.

He believed in equality. At one time a Jewish merchant, Levi Beck, wished to open a store in Saltcoats. Many were sufficiently prejudiced to endeavor to prevent this. Allan MacLeod was enraged. He brought his considerable influence to bear and the protestors were silenced. Levi Beck's store became a great benefit to the community.

Among all the Gaelic speaking emigrants, Allan MacLeod of Stornoway, Island of Lewis, stood out as an exemplary citizen.

Allan and Mary (Stewart) MacLeod, parents of Malcolm McLeod, Yorkton, SK, 1938.

A STORY ABOUT A BOY

The Boy lived in a household full of children. There were two older brothers, two older sisters, the Boy and a four-year-old brother.

The Boy was fair skinned with blue eyes so light that in winter they blinked white as the reflected snow. He was extremely bright and innovative and very energetic. His younger brother was his constant companion. They romped, played games and caused mayhem in the family; together they played tricks on the older brothers who had definite responsibilities around the home, especially in the barnyard where they cared for all the animals.

The calves and young livestock were the younger boys' easy prey. When they found a calf lying down, it was soon aroused by two bodies on its back. It made a valiant effort to get its two hind legs up and always tumbled the boys together onto the ground as it rose, no matter how hard they endeavored to stay astride. Great adventure!

They took ropes from the barn and tried to lasso the calves. This harassed the cows, concerned for their calves, as well as the older brothers, who had to restore order in the barnyard.

The most fun in winter, on a cold day, was to crawl into the straw stack where the old sow had burrowed a deep tunnel to keep her brood warm. [They would] chase the pigs out and take over the warm spot. This caused laundry problems for the sisters, as this family took great pride in its cleanliness. The mother shook her head, scolded and went back to tending the baby.

The father was a religious man, so immediately after the evening meal, he read from the Scriptures, mostly Old Testament, not likely to hold the attention of two restless little boys. After, all knelt by their chairs as he proceeded to pronounce a long Levitical prayer.

What better time to poke big brother with a pointed stick, conveniently tucked in a pocket, or to tweak a braid or make funny faces at the younger oldest sister?

Squirming or giggling was severely reprimanded if you were caught. The little boys were cautious.

The parents were hospitable and generous and grownups often visited in the afternoons. They were treated to the blackest tea, with lots of cream and sugar, accompanied by scones or barley cakes with homemade jam.

Among the most frequent visitors were the minister and his wife. They were in midlife and childless, which in those days was thought of as a disadvantage. Somewhere, sometime, a deal was made between them and the Boy's parents. The Boy was told he was going to live with the Minister.

In his new home he was completely desolate. The house was sterile and quiet; no one to play with, no one to tease, no calves, no dogs, no pigs. Just two oldish people, strict and proper, always admonishing. How he hated it.

At night he beat his pillow in fury and wept himself to sleep, over and over repeating, "They gave me away, they gave me away". Daytime he resented the English lessons. Why didn't they speak his Gaelic language? He knew they spoke it in church and with his parents. As long as he lived, he would hate those people or anyone with the same name.

One mild afternoon the Minister hitched his horses to the cutter and he and his wife took the Boy to go visiting with them. Imagine his joy when they approached his married sister's homestead. A short time before she had married a fine young newcomer, a veteran of the Boer War.

As they were welcomed into the cozy little kitchen by his pretty sister, white aproned and rosy cheeked, who greeted him so lovingly, he made a resolution. He couldn't bear it anymore. He was going home.

He slipped unnoticed out of the door, ran around the side of the house and headed for the lane. He knew how to go home from here. He had been here many times before. When he reached the road, hard packed with old snow, walking was easy. He was on his way! He was alone! He was going home!

No living creature was in site. He was not afraid. Wolves would not harm him and what else was there to be afraid of? Once in a while a prairie chicken was startled out of her resting place or a cottontail would cross his path.

He watched for landmarks, being sure to turn the right way at road crossings. He trudged on and on. His sturdy little legs began to ache; his boots grew heavy and his mittens were dampening as he wiped the tears that would come, or the nose that would drip, but his little heart was stout.

When he reached his father's lane, more than four miles from where he had started, the sun was making long shadows on the snow and he was walking slowly. He was tired and apprehensive.

The dogs ran to greet him, jumping on his shoulders and licking his tear stained face. He shoved them down with a tentative pat. No one was out as he approached the house. He went silently up the steps and opened the door. The crowded kitchen and warm familiar smells almost overcame him.

There were exclamations of surprise and a question from every mouth, "Who brought you here"? "How did you get here."

"I walked home from my sister's and I will not go back to that Minister's house again."

His father looked at the strong, sturdy, self-confident child, rose and removed the boots, coat, cap, scarf and soggy mittens, and setting him on a chair, rubbed the muscles of the weary legs, patted the tousled head and ordered the sister "bring hot soup".

The mother handed the baby to a sister, went to the Boy, gently shook a disapproving head, then as the tears came, wrapped her arms around the longing child. There was a hubbub of joy and all were laughing together.

The Father said a short prayer of thanksgiving, they silently resolved that never again would he permit any one to persuade him to give up one of his children.

The Boy grew and became the most dependable, productive and ambitious son in the family.

Editors' Note. Malcolm recounted events about his childhood to Janet. The story "About a Boy" is the result.

Janet believed Malcolm's parents, prosperous farmers, had no need to lighten an economic burden by "adopting out" one of their children, a custom common in that era. She thought they were convinced to do so by the minister who wielded the greatest of influence in the Scotch community. He saw the intelligence and energy in four-year-old Malcolm, and determined to give him, not unselfishly so, all the advantages that would come from being the son of the minister. Malcolm's parents, not wanting to deny their gifted child this opportunity, and highly respecting the minister, acquiesced, most probably reluctantly so.

One wonders at the regret they felt afterward; Janet said the incident was never mentioned to her by anyone in the Allan MacLeod family. And Malcolm himself did not speak of this, even to Janet, until he was seventy-five years old.

THE STORY OF MY LIFE

THE STORY OF MY LIFE

By Janet McLeod

What is lovely and of good report, to paraphrase the Apostle Paul, is all I wish to write of memories of my life.

The first thing I remember is white, glistening snow and the advent of my sister Phemie. I was three and it was January and the winter was very long in 1904.

Spring came and I remember being very happy playing among the Croci in the soft green grass. I sang a lot. My father called me "Baby Edith with the golden hair", and was affectionate to me. I sat on his knee and when I was older, I remember him reciting what he remembered of the Shorter Catechism and also snatches of Psalms. He also knew a lot of Evangelical Hymns, parts of which I still recall.

Life was isolated and lonely. A few people came by on their way to town.

My second sister, Beth, was born when I was seven and had started school. I walked the three miles with my brothers Colin, ten and Alex, twelve. There were no more than ten or twelve students.

The same map of Canada hung on the wall as long as I attended. I still see it. I learned a lot by staring at it. The shape of the Great Lakes is indelibly stamped on my mind. The aluminum painted stove was a complete eye sore planted in the middle of the room. I was on the wrong side of it and couldn't see out of the windows.

By the time I was nine, my brother Alex was preparing for the Grade Eight Exam. He was the first in the District to take it.

Listening to the eighth-grade study literature introduced me to poetry. I loved parts of "To a Skylark", and learned to love Keats and Shelly. I don't remember doing much other school work.

When I was thirteen, Colin and I wrote our Eighth Grade Exam, and both passed. I am grateful to my parents to this day. That certificate opened the door to the outside world for me.

High School was six miles away, so that first year, Colin drove the team to Bredenbury for School every day. In winter, it was a long drive. Next year I boarded with a fine Danish Lady in Churchbridge to take grade ten. Believe it or not, Home Economics was introduced that year even though the school had no equipment.

For the next two years, I lived with my cousin Percy Ross and his wife Jen and went to the Winnipeg Collegiate Institute.

My brother Forbes was born in 1914 and that was a surprise which brought me much pleasure.

In 1915 my brother Alex enlisted in the army and was killed at Vimy Ridge in 1917. War fever was high and grain prices were up, but there were no young men around. One of my cousins was killed and my cousin's husband.

After Normal School, I was offered a school in the Eden School District, Malcolm's family's District, twelve miles north of Saltcoats. I taught for a year and a half and gave it up for marriage. That was a permanent position and I have had a very full life. My husband and children filled my days. There was much joy, and much grief but we produced a marvelous family.

Now I live alone. I miss my life long companion very much but I am secure in the knowledge that I am surrounded by love and caring people and if I could, I would still sing as I once did, "I love the lord, for He is good. I praise God's name".

Editors' Note. This was written for a writing class Janet took sometime in the late nineteen eighties.

Janet and Malcolm McLeod,
Elizabeth and Jack Ross, 1919.

Janet and Malcolm McLeod, 1920.

Janet and Malcolm McLeod, 1948.

BIOGRAPHY

Janet Edith Rose Mary Ann Ross, as she was named at birth, was born on January 16, 1901 in the British Northwest Territories of Canada. Educated to be a teacher, she graduated from Winnipeg Collegiate, attended Central Normal School and taught in a country school before her marriage to Malcolm McLeod. They settled in Mountain Park, Alberta, where John Alexander, Mary Maxine and Elizabeth Leila were born. They moved to the Detroit area, eventually settling on several acres in Erin Township. Allan Malcolm, Jean Elaine, Janet Edith, Margaret Christine and Karen Isabelle were born in Michigan. Another infant, twin to Jean Elaine, died shortly after birth, and Elizabeth Leila died in young adulthood.

Janet raised her children and helped her husband make a good life for their family, while also pursing her own intellectual interests. Her tastes in literature ran from Shakespeare to Toni Morrison. Her favorite music was classical, but she enjoyed every type, and often hummed hymns while working. She sewed much of her daughters' clothing and became adept at changing a pattern to suit their whims. Her English style gardens at the Big House on Common Road, which she planned and planted, were beautiful and abundant. Items she crocheted and embroidered are still in existence, and at the age of eighty-five, she taught herself the skill and completed a counted cross stitch piece. She canned, and later froze, much of what her husband grew in the garden, and in the very early days, thought nothing of "harvesting" a chicken for dinner. She was more chef than cook, open to trying new ingredients and cooking techniques; she did algorithms in her head for amusement, and read, memorized, recited or wrote poetry most days of her life.

Janet loved her sisters and brothers, and often related stories of their growing up together. She learned the value of family ties while living a rather isolated life, with her siblings as her main companions. It was important to her that her own children remained close as adults, connected not only by blood, but by friendship. Her eight children didn't disappoint; as adults, in spite of occasional differences, the 'ties that bind', stretched but never came close to breaking. The sisters and brothers looked and still look to each other for friendship and support.

A lifelong Presbyterian, Janet was a progressive Christian, and one of the first women Elders ordained in the Presbytery of Detroit. In addition to being an elder, she taught Sunday School, and was President of the Woman's Association at Erin Church, attending the Biennial Meeting as an official delegate.

Human rights, civil rights and women's rights were causes dear to her and she was an early member of the National Organization of Women, working for the passage of the Equal Rights Amendment. A lifelong Democrat, she believed in the dignity and innate goodness of all human beings.

In her middle fifties, she studied at Wayne State University to get her Michigan teaching certification and become a substitute teacher.

Janet was very hospitable. The phrase "put the kettle on" was used to welcome almost everyone who came to her door. As a result, her children were raised in a happy, bustling household, where laughter, chatter, singing, or playing on the big black piano, were often background noises.

To say Janet was proud of her children is to state the obvious. When the young couple and their family emigrated from Mt. Park, Alberta to Detroit, Michigan, her dream was that each of them would at least graduate from high school. Suffice to say that Elgar's 'Pomp and Circumstance' became her favorite piece of music. She heard it played at eight high school graduations and many, many more times as she lived to see her children, and grandchildren attain more educational goals than she ever dreamed. Indeed, "Education is an easy thing to carry" was not an empty Ross motto.

Janet was born before there was travel by air, and lived well past the day man walked on the moon. In spite of the deep, devastating loss of her daughter Elizabeth, and Elizabeth's husband and children, a tragedy that could have made her bitter, she chose to dwell in the light. The majority of her life was lived with purpose and with an abiding sense of joyfulness. And, to paraphrase the Psalmist, as she often did, she gave thanks to the Lord, because she felt, His faithful love surrounded her all of her life.

CHILDREN OF JANET AND MALCOLM McLEOD

Janet Ross 1901-1992
married Malcolm McLeod 1898-1980

John Alexander 1920-2001
Mary Maxine (Foster) 1923-2004
Elizabeth Leila (Nott) 1925-1949
Allan Malcolm 1927-1995
Janet Edith 1928-1928
Jean Elaine (Blake) 1928
Janet Edith (Michel) 1934-2008
Margaret Christine (Ebert) 1937
Karen Isabelle (Cox) 1943

Top row, left to right: Janet; Janet (mother); Malcolm; Karen; Elaine; Maxine; John. Kneeling: Margaret; Allan. Alma College, 1956.

Janet and Lovey, 1989.

ACKNOWLEDGEMENTS

Thank you to Sandra Vasher, daughter, niece and cousin to the clan by her marriage to John Malcolm McLeod Cox. She is a true McLeod at heart, and a writer, like Janet. Without her encouragement, knowledge and expertise, this book would never have become a reality.

Thank you to Joseph Cox, for helping us every step of the way.

And to everyone else who helped; It took a small Clan of McLeods from Arizona, to North Carolina to Michigan to Ontario to bring this project to life. Janet would be pleased.

Mortal Ink Press Heritage is an imprint of
Mortal Ink Press, LLC, an indie publishing
company owned and operated by Sandra L. Vasher.
Mortal Ink Press Heritage helps
families record and publish their legacies.

Contact Sandra Vasher at
publisher@mortalinkpress.com or visit
our website to learn more.

https://mortalinkpress.com/heritage

www.ingramcontent.com/pod-product-compliance
Lightning Source LLC
Chambersburg PA
CBHW030156100526
44592CB00009B/298